GROWTH MINDSET BOOK FOR KIDS

PRETTY PICKLES

THIS BOOK BELONGS TO

_____

PRETTY PICKLES

ALL ABOUT ME

AGE:

FAVOURITE SPORT:

MOST SKILLED AT:

MOST CONFIDENCE IN:

GOALS:

PRETTY PICKLES

DAY 1:
MY ACCOMPLISHMENT BOX

MY PROUDEST ACCOMPLISHMENTS

• •

• •

• •

• •

• •

• •

PRETTY PICKLES

DAY 2:

I CAN LEARN	I CAN LEARN
I CAN LEARN	**I CAN LEARN**

PRETTY PICKLES

DAY 3:
TRAIN THE BRAIN

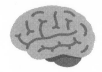

Things I should tell myself	Things I should not tell myself
i.e. Making mistakes is ok! I can learn from them.	*i.e. I made a mistake so I can't do it.*

PRETTY PICKLES

DAY 4:
LEARNING FROM
MISTAKES

MISTAKE I'VE MADE:

WHAT IT TAUGHT ME:

MISTAKE I'VE MADE:

WHAT IT TAUGHT ME:

PRETTY PICKLES

DAY 4:
LEARNING FROM
MISTAKES

MISTAKE I'VE MADE:

_____

WHAT IT TAUGHT ME:

_____

MISTAKE I'VE MADE:

_____

WHAT IT TAUGHT ME:

_____

PRETTY PICKLES

DAY 5:
LOVING MISTAKES

The best thing about making mistakes is...

Next time I make a mistake I will...

DAY 6:
'I CAN'
AFFIRMATIONS

i.e. I can do anything, I can solve problems

DAY 7:
MY SUPER POWERS

Things I'm really good at

DAY 8:
Q&A WITH MY
FAVOURITE PEOPLE

Your family or friends may know your greatest strengths even if you don't. Ask them.

 Person to interview:

_____

? What are things I'm good at?

_____

? When have you seen me at my best?

_____

? Can you give me some examples of when I'm at my best?

_____

PRETTY PICKLES

DAY 8:
Q&A WITH MY
FAVOURITE PEOPLE

Your family or friends may know your greatest strengths even if you don't. Ask them.

 Person to interview:

? What are things I'm good at?

? When have you seen me at my best?

? Can you give me some examples of when I'm at my best?

DAY 8:
Q&A WITH MY
FAVOURITE PEOPLE

Your family or friends may know your greatest strengths even if you don't. Ask them.

 Person to interview:

_____

? What are things I'm good at?

_____

? When have you seen me at my best?

_____

? Can you give me some examples of when I'm at my best?

_____

PRETTY PICKLES

DAY 9:
GROWTH MINDSET
TIC TAC TOE

Grab a friend of family member and play a game of Tic Tac Toe. Each time you place a 'x' or 'o', do the activity in the box.

Write a 'I can' statement	Tell someone about your goal(s)	Shout out: 'I can do anything!'
List 3 things you want to learn	List 3 things you're good at	Complete the sentence: I love learning about...
Finish this: Mistakes are great because...	Tell someone about your goal(s)	List 3 things you want to learn
Shout out: 'I can do anything!'	Write a 'I can' statement	Write an affirmation

PRETTY PICKLES

DAY 9:
GROWTH MINDSET
TIC TAC TOE

Play another game, just for fun. =)

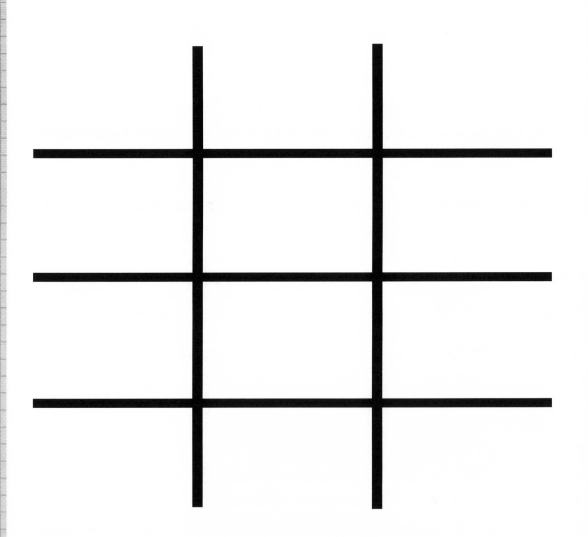

PRETTY PICKLES

DAY 10:
AT MY BEST

Some things like getting a good night's rest of having a healthy breakfast bring out the best in us. What are some things you need to be at your best?

I'm at my best when...

i.e. I've eaten breakfast before 9am

_____

_____

_____

_____

_____

_____

PRETTY PICKLES

DAY 11:
MY MORNING ROUTINE

Having a routine can help you start the day right. Come up with a morning routine that will bring out your best self.

First thing I'll do when I wake up is...

_____

First thing I'll do when I wake up is...

_____

_____

_____

_____

DAY 12:
WHAT I LEARNED TODAY

Everyday is a new opportunity to learn
something new. What did you learn today?

PRETTY PICKLES

DAY 12:
BOOKS I WANT TO READ

Books are a great way to help us grow. Make your reading list.

• •

• •

• •

• •

• •

• •

DAY 12:
BOOKS I WANT TO READ

Books are a great way to help us grow. Make your reading list.

· ·

· ·

· ·

· ·

· ·

· ·

DAY 13:
MY MENTOR

Having mentors in our lives can help us become the best version of yourself. Think abotu the people in your life who could be a mentor.

Name:

This mentor would make a good mentor because...

DAY 14:
WHEN I GROW UP...

You can be anything, anyone you want to be.

When I grow up I want to be...

DAY 15:
YOUR SUPER HERO POWERS

Discover your inner super hero.

My super hero name:

My super hero power:

My powers come from:

When you need me, just...

DAY 16:
WORDS ABOUT YOU

List some words that describe you. Check with your family and friends to see if they have any words to add.

DAY 17:
WHAT MAKES YOU UNIQUE

There are things you do that make you unique. Can you think of a few of them?

What makes me unique is...

What makes me unique is...

What makes me unique is...

What makes me unique is...

PRETTY PICKLES

DAY 17:
WHAT MAKES YOU
UNIQUE

What makes me unique is...

What makes me unique is...

What makes me unique is...
There are things you do that make you
unique. Can you think of a few of them?

What makes me unique is...

DAY 19:
THINGS THAT ARE
IMPORTANT TO ME

List the people and things you value most.

DAY 20:
WHAT I LOVE ABOUT ME

List as many things as you can.

DAY 20:
WHAT I LOVE ABOUT ME

List as many things as you can.

PRETTY PICKLES

DAY 21:
A LETTER TO YOUR FUTURE SELF

Write a letter to your older self. What would you want your future self to know? Tell them about your life right now and where you see your life in 5 years.

DAY 21:
A LETTER TO YOUR FUTURE SELF CONT...

_____

_____

_____

_____

_____

_____

_____

PRETTY PICKLES

DAY 22: GRATITUDE

What are some things you're thankful for?

DAY 24:
THINGS YOU'RE PROUD OF

What are some things you've accomplished that make you proud?

PRETTY PICKLES

DAY 25:
TACKLING CHALLENGES

We all face challenges. Whether it's solving a puzzle or taking an exam, we need to keep going. What are some things you'll tell yourself to tackle on any challenge with confidence?

DAY 25:
TACKLING CHALLENGES
CONT...

PRETTY PICKLES

DAY 26:
THANK YOU LETTERS

Think about the people you love most. How have they helped you? Are you thankful for the people in your life? Write them a thank you note.

DEAR . . .

DAY 26:
THANK YOU LETTERS CONT

DEAR...

DAY 27:
WHAT YOU LEARNED

Every day we learn something new. What did you learn this week?

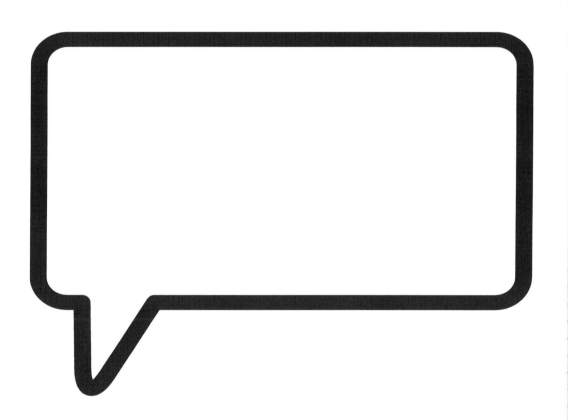

PRETTY PICKLES

DAY 28:
CHALLENGES

Think about a challenge you've had to
overcome. How did you get through it?

Challenge I had to overcome:

_____

_____

Things I did to overcome the challenge:

_____

_____

What I learned:

_____

_____

PRETTY PICKLES

DAY 29:
THE ULTIMATE GOAL

Think about something you really want to achieve. Now work out how you can reach your goal.

 My goal:

 Steps to take to achieve it:

 I would like to reach the goal by...

PRETTY PICKLES

DAY 30: REFLECTION

Think about all the things you've learned about yourself from doing the exercises.

Things I've learned:

_____

_____

_____

_____

_____

_____

PRETTY PICKLES

EXTRAS

Draw your dream life

PRETTY PICKLES

EXTRAS

Draw a self-portrait

EXTRAS

Ask a friend to draw a portrait of you.
Compare it to your own drawing.

Made in the USA
Monee, IL
13 May 2020